Come Sit with Me Again
Sermons for Children

Don-Paul Benjamin and Ron Miner

Illustrated by
Don-Paul Benjamin

The Pilgrim Press
Cleveland, Ohio

Acknowledgments

Without the assistance and inspiration of many people, this book would not have been possible. Special thanks and love to John Dennis and Erwin Barrow.

The Pilgrim Press, Cleveland Ohio, 44115
© 1987 The Pilgrim Press

The biblical quotation in this book is from the Revised Standard Version of the Bible, copyright 1946, 1952, and © 1971, 1973 by the Division of Christian Education, National Council of Churches, and is used by permission.

97 96 95 94 93 92   5 4 3 2

Library of Congress Cataloging-in-Publication Data

Benjamin, Don-Paul, 1945-
Come sit with me again.

1. Children's sermons. I. Miner, Ron, 1938-
II. Title.
BV4315.B355   1987   252'.53 86-30588
ISBN 0-8298-0748-9 (pbk.)

Contents

Preface

The gratifying response to our first book of sermons for children plus our own continued growth as Christians and as educators, has inspired this second book. It, like its predecessor, was guided by our belief that children should be included in the worship service and by our conviction that sermons for children touch not only children, but also the child in each of us.

This new set of sermons continues the popular format of our first book. We have included a few more daring events such as filling the sanctuary with a fusillade of buzzing balloons to dramatize the thrill of Pentecost and shouting in church to accent the joy of Easter. We have also incorporated a new section that features activities based on the teachings of Jesus. Our expanded special events section includes new sermons for major holidays, with emphases on Christmas and Easter.

Introduction

The future of the church we know and love lies in the younger generation, but all too often we fail to include the children at Sunday morning worship services. Children too need to hear—on their own level—the message of God's love for all people.

The sermons in this book are designed to appeal to children four to eight years old, but other children may participate. With appropriate modification, many of these sermons can be used for older youth. But everyone enters the sanctuary on Sunday morning as a child. If worship can involve the child in each of us, it is likely that the adult will be led to a personal relationship with God as well. One's age has nothing to do with ability to respond to the simple beauty of God's love. Were it otherwise, the parables of Jesus would never have survived.

Jesus called out to children that the disciples had sent away, and he declared: "Let the children come to me, and do not hinder them; for to such belongs the kingdom of God. Truly, I say to you, whoever does not receive the kingdom of God like a child shall not enter it [Luke 18:16–17]." The implications are twofold: (1) children do have a place in the Christian worship service and (2) a "sermon" or other presentation geared to children will remind everyone—adults included—of the beauty and simplicity of Christ's message.

Giving children's sermons can be a personal and intensely rewarding way to share the reality of Christian love. One can enjoy great freedom in presenting a brief experience to children. Having entered the sanctuary on stilts, skipped rope before the congregation, and blown soap bubbles in the house of God, we have experienced that freedom.

One hazard of putting these sermons in book form is that readers might think that these pages cover all the good ideas. But each person who fingers these pages has a background of his or her own unique holy experiences. Share those experiences in a way that is comfortable to you, and you will have enriched more than one life. Present them from the child in you to the "children" around you, and you will have given a children's sermon. Use the freedom you have to lead children of all ages to discover God's love in the world in which they live.

The children's sermons in this book were adapted from activities that took place on the chancel floor of the First Presbyterian Church in Corvallis, Oregon. The children are called forward about twenty minutes into the service. They sit on the floor with their backs to the congregation, and the leader sits on the floor with them. This establishes a sense of intimacy. A quality hand-held microphone is essential for the success of this system, because the rest of the congregation should be included. In a few weeks the children will be used to speaking into the microphone.

At the end of each sermon are noted "Materials" (prop/s needed) and "Scripture References" (thoughts for meditation) for use by the leader in preparing for the sermons.

The lesson plan for each sermon includes five basic steps:

1. *Motivation:* A presentation of materials, props, or concepts related to the sermon to set the stage and inspire interest.

2. *Activity:* A tangible experience in which the children can participate. The activity establishes a concrete basis for further discussion.

3. *Guided Discussion:* A period of discussion guided by the sermon leader. Includes key questions for the children to consider and anticipated responses.

4. *Leader Message:* A "script" for the leader with suggested statements. The message is designed to relate the children's experiences and discussion to Christian life.

5. *Closing Prayer:* A simple prayer that acknowledges the role of God in the topic of the session.

At the end of the sermon, the children may be dismissed to an alternate activity or to return to their families.

Who dares write sermons for children? The child in each of us shares with the child in you, the reader. In sharing, we celebrate our freedom to seek peace and un-

8

derstanding, and to "enter the kingdom," as children. This freedom comes from the children of God who touch our lives on a regular basis—Sara, Kate, Fred, Betty, Lena, Alice, Warren, Mary, Gene, John, Wendy, Erwin, Kay, Sharon, Leonard, Carol, Harold, Cindy, Marcia—and all other childlike souls who have shared themselves with Don-Paul and Ron.

A Question of Balance

Motivation: The leader displays two balance beams that are placed parallel to each other, a short distance apart.

Activity: The leader takes a position at one end of the beams and the children stand at the other end. A few children—one child at a time—are invited to walk along either beam toward the leader. Some may be successful, but most will have trouble. After a few solo tries, the leader has one child stand on each beam and three children stand on the floor—one between the beams and one on either side of the beams. The five children stand side by side facing the leader. The two children on the beams are instructed to place their hands on the shoulders of the children next to them (or to join hands). This group of five is invited to walk slowly forward from one end of the beam to the other. The beams are then put aside and the children are assembled for discussion.

Guided Discussion:	Why was it so difficult to walk the beam alone? (Had to keep your balance. Too narrow. No one to help us if we start to fall.)
Leader Message:	The path that Jesus asks us to follow is a narrow one and a difficult one. Being a Christian is hard work, but luckily we have help in the form of other Christians. I'd like the entire congregation to stand and join hands. Now, children, look at that wonderful sight! Can you see how a united church can help us all walk the Christian path together?
Closing Prayer:	We thank you, God, for those around us. They support us when we begin to fall. They encourage us when we are discouraged. And they guide us when we are lost. Be with us as we offer our hands to others who need help. Make us alert to opportunities to walk with all your people. Amen.
Materials:	Two low balance beams. These might be obtained from a local school. Two 4×4 fence posts will serve. If there is a concern about safety, qualified adults might be recruited to perform in place of the children.
Scripture Reference:	John 15:11–17

Welcome Workers

Motivation: The leader displays the help-wanted pages from a local newspaper.

Activity: The leader announces that he/she has just been reading about work. The children are invited to talk about work they do at home.

Guided Discussion: What sort of work do you do at home? (Various answers.) What would happen to the house (yard, animals, farm, etc.) if you didn't do your work? (House would get dirty. Animals would go hungry. Etc.)

Leader
Message: There are many kinds of work in our
            world. Everywhere we look there are cer-
            tain things that must be done. Just think,
            for example, of all the work needed to
            keep our church going. (Give examples as
            applicable.) Today we are going to wel-
            come (some new officers, a new music di-
            rector, some new teachers, a new
            groundskeeper, etc.) to our church. (Ex-
            plain a bit about what the new people do.)
            They are joining our church family and
            their special work will help make our
            church a healthier, happier, more produc-
            tive place. I hope that after the service
            each of you will say hello to our new work-
            ers and welcome them to our church and
            wish them well in their important work.

Closing
Prayer: How wonderful it is, God, that there are
            so many ways to serve you. Accept each of
            us with the skills we have. Help us to see
            and appreciate the special work of those
            around us and help us to express our
            thanks for the gifts that others devote to
            your service. Amen.

Materials: The want ad section of a newspaper

*Scripture
References:*   1 Corinthians 12:12–31; Romans 12:4–8

Partly Cloudy

Motivation: The leader stretches out on his/her back, staring at the sanctuary ceiling and invites the children to do the same.

Activity: At the leader's direction, the children are asked to pretend that they are outside on a warm sunny day, staring up into the blue sky and watching clouds float by. The leader asks the children to imagine the shapes they see in the clouds and to describe what they see. The leader may have to encourage imagery by such phrases as, "I imagine a cloud in the shape of a lion with a long, white, billowing mane." After a bit of such activity, the leader sits up and invites the children to do the same.

Guided
Discussion: What is a cloud made of? (Cotton. Air. Moisture. Rain. Other ideas.) If we were to look closely—depending on the time of year and the air temperature—we would see that a cloud is made up of millions of

tiny drops of water, or sometimes tiny pieces of ice. Because clouds are so far away, all the drops seem to join together to make those beautiful floating shapes that we see on bright blue days. I'll tell you a secret about something special I think about when I see clouds. I like to think of clouds as churches in the sky: each of us; you and I and all the people out there (indicating congregation) and all the choir members and everyone in the church all join together like those tiny drops of water to form something beautiful. We join together in worship to form something bright and wonderful. I hope the next time you look up at the clouds you'll think about how all of us, and all of you, join together to form this church into a special place.

Closing Prayer:	Your world amazes us, O God. From tiny drops of water a cloud is formed. From individual Christians a church is formed. Open our minds to the power of your creative and unifying love. Amen.
Materials:	None required, although the leader may consider stimulating the children's imagination by providing cloud pictures or even a blue bit of cardboard with clouds represented by cotton fluffs. A sermon such as this would be quite appropriate for an outdoor service.
Scripture Reference:	Hebrews 12:1

Tender Tape

Motivation: The leader introduces a paramedic. The children are assured that the leader is not really injured. But they are asked to pretend that the leader has broken his/her pointer finger playing softball.

Activity: The children are invited to watch closely as the paramedic splints and tapes the leader's index/pointer finger and middle finger neatly together. They are instructed to think about why two fingers are being taped when only one is injured.

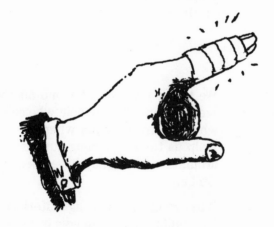

Guided
Discussion: Why are two fingers taped when only the pointer finger is broken? (Various answers. It is hoped that someone will suggest the concept of using the good finger to guide the healing of the broken one.)

Leader	
Message:	A broken finger won't heal properly without help from its neighbor. Left on its own, without being joined to the sturdy neighbor, the broken finger will not mend properly. It will be crooked and useless. It needs help to heal and grow properly. Sometimes our lives and our dreams are broken, much like we might break a finger or an arm or a leg. At times like these we need to heal and we need the support of our neighbors and friends. We also need the support and closeness of the church and of God. Bound together like these two fingers, our friends, our church, and our faith in God can help us mend and heal properly. The act of joining together with other Christians can help us through painful times.

Closing	
Prayer:	We thank you, God, for one another. We are surrounded by people who care for us when we are sick and when we are well. Help us to be a healing support to those around us when they have special needs. Amen.

Materials: Bandaging and splinting materials applied by a uniformed paramedic or nurse.

Scripture
Reference: Matthew 9:18–38

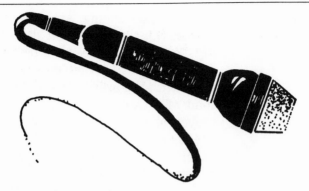

Famous Last Words

Motivation: The leader produces a tape recorder and announces that the voices of the congregation in prayer have been recorded.

Activity: The leader invites the children to listen to the recording and think about which word said in the prayer is the most important.

Guided
Discussion: The leader puts the recorder aside and asks the children which word is the most important. (Answers will vary.)

Leader
Message: Whenever I pray, or when I hear a prayer, I like to think that the most important word is the one at the end: amen. Some people think that amen means "the end," or "that's all." It has a much deeper and

more special meaning. Amen means "yes"; "certainly"; "in truth"; "let it be so." We say "Amen" at the close of a prayer not as an ending, but to show that we strongly agree with the prayer's message. You can think of it this way: we bow our heads in prayer, and at the end we nod our heads (leader nods head in agreement) to say: "Yes, God! Yes, Jesus! Let it be so! Let it happen!" When we say "Amen," we close each prayer with a word that clearly states our faith in the power of that prayer.

Closing
Prayer:

Dear God, it is such a joy to talk to you and know we are heard. As we pray, we pray from our hearts, knowing you will answer in our hearts. Let us all say: Amen.

Materials:

A tape recorder and a cassette. It might be best to record the congregation on a previous occasion so that last-minute technical problems do not spoil the product. A recording of the Lord's Prayer would be appropriate, since it is of short duration and the children will already be familiar with the words.

Scripture
Reference:

1 Corinthians 14:13–19

Hearing Is Believing

Motivation: The leader asks the children to sit in silence and listen for a full minute.

Activity: After the silent listening, the leader invites children to come forward quietly, one at a time, whisper to the leader what they heard, and then quietly return to their seats.

Guided
Discussion: What sounds did we hear? (Reports will vary: someone coughing, cars passing by, birds singing, the heater/air conditioner, people talking, etc.) Were the sounds loud or soft? (Answers will vary, but most children will probably report that the sounds were soft.)

Leader	
Message:	Unless we listen closely and carefully, sometimes we miss things. When the (organ, piano, etc.) plays, or when the choir sings, the sounds ring through the church with joy and thunder and feeling. But some other sounds that we make in church are just as pleasing to God and just as powerful. Now if you listen again, carefully, you will hear one of the most powerful sounds I know: the sound of prayer. I want you to listen closely as the congregation softly prays the Lord's Prayer. (To the congregation): Let us pray together softly. (Lead the group in softly praying.) Amen. Did you feel the energy from that prayer? What a blessing!
Closing Prayer:	Help us, dear God, to hear those special sounds that warm the heart and strengthen the spirit. May the sound of prayer serve as a melody of inspiration and a theme that guides our lives. Amen.
Materials:	None, although a word of explanation in the bulletin as to what is expected of the congregation might be helpful.
Scripture References:	Revelation 8:1; 1 Kings 19:12; Psalm 46:10

A Reed Indeed

Motivation: The leader invites the children to watch
               closely as a reed instrument player per-
               forms directly in front of them.

Activity: To stimulate interest and ensure close at-
               tention, the children are instructed to try
               to imitate each of the musician's move-
               ments as he/she performs. As the children
               watch and mimic his/her actions, the mu-
               sician first blows into the instrument and
               then expresses surprise and confusion
               when no sound is made (the mouthpiece/
               reed is not present). The musician
               scratches his/her head, looks about, finds
               the mouthpiece/reed, inserts it, and blows
               a few notes. He/she bows and exits.

Guided
Discussion: Why didn't the instrument make a sound
               at first? (A piece or a part was missing.
               Some children may name the mouthpiece/
               reed as the missing item.) What happened
               when the mouthpiece/reed was added? (It
               made music. Made a sound. Worked.)

Leader
Message: (Showing a reed.) This is a reed. It's a
               strip of wood (or metal) that vibrates
               when you blow on it. Without this small
               strip of material, the instrument we saw

won't make its lovely sound. The reed is a tiny but necessary part of many musical instruments. Without the reed the instrument is silent. With the reed our breath is transformed into a beautiful, almost magical sound. I like to think of the reed in the same way that I think of prayer. Every day we say lots of words, but the beauty of those words is never more special than when they are used in prayer. Words said in prayer make a beautiful music, a music God loves.

Closing Prayer:

We are inspired, O God, by the simple reed. This slender bit of material is so critical to the sound of music. Our prayers are like reeds. Without the music of prayer our lives are silent and empty. Fill our lives with the joyous song of your love. Amen.

Materials:

Any of a number of woodwind or reed instruments could be used: bassoon, oboe, English horn, clarinet, saxophone, or flute. Depending on what is available, use whichever term is more appropriate—mouthpiece or reed. The separate reed can be from any instrument. The reed itself, not the mouthpiece, should be displayed during the "Leader Message." It might add emphasis to the sermon if the musician could be a guest artist for the day, having already performed for the congregation before the children assemble.

Scripture Reference:

Psalm 150

High-Grade Oar

Motivation: The leader displays an oar.

Activity: The children are invited to show how this object is used.

Guided
Discussion: Why do we use an oar? How is it helpful? (Moves a boat over the water. Makes us go faster. Helps us steer. Helps us paddle.) What would happen if we were out in a boat and lost our oar? (We would stop. We'd have to get it back. We'd be in trouble. We'd just drift around. We might sink. We'd get lost.)

Leader
Message: I like to think of the Bible as an oar: something that—if we use it properly—helps us keep our lives on course, helps us move ahead, helps us steer. The more we know about using an oar, the better we become at rowing and steering a boat. The more we know the Bible, the better we become at guiding our way through life. With the Bible, we know God's will and we are in control. With the Bible, we are rowing—not drifting.

Closing	
Prayer:	God, your love is our oar. Your word leads us safely through the troubles of this world. Help us to use the Bible to guide our lives and move us closer to you. Without you we are lost. Guide our efforts to use your word with greater skill. Amen.
Materials:	An oar.
Scripture	
References:	1 Peter 1:10–16; Deuteronomy 6:1–3a

In the Cards

Motivation: The leader passes out several colorful baseball cards to the children.

Activity: The leader invites two or three children to tell about their cards. (This is a catcher and he plays for New York, etc.)

Guided
Discussion: Why do you think these particular people have their pictures on these cards? (Famous. Good players. Heroes. Stars.) What do you have to do to get your picture on a baseball card? (Be famous. Hit home runs. Play well. Win the series.) (The leader may wish to collect the cards before presenting the message.)

Leader
Message: Heroes come and go. People who were famous to your grandparents may be unknown today. Even people who were famous when I was a child might not get a second glance if they visited your school. Men and women are famous for a short time and then, often, they are forgotten.

But some men and women are remembered for hundreds, even thousands, of years. They are the people of the Old Testament. I wonder, if we were to make a set of cards like these for Old Testament heroes, who should appear on them? (The leader may ask for suggestions from the children, drawing out names and accomplishments that the children associate with each. Or the leader may wish to list some of those suggested in the remainder of the message. A combination of the children's nominations and those of the leader might be fruitful, although the leader should be prepared—if he/she elects the nominations route—for some inaccuracies from the children, such as one young boy's recollection that Noah invented the dictionary.) Certainly Noah would have a card. After all, he was chosen by God to gather his family and all the animals into the ark in preparation for the Great Flood. And Joseph, who kept faith and whom God did not abandon even though Joseph was sold into slavery. And what about Ruth, whose kindness to her mother-in-law made her seem an angel on earth? Or Moses, to whom the ten commandments were entrusted? Or Hannah, who gave her most precious gift, her son Samuel, to the service of God? And what about Daniel, who was willing to face the lions rather than stop praying to God, and Esther, who saved her people with her faith? And David, who was strong in battle and wrote beautiful psalms? Or Isaiah and the other prophets, who foretold Christ's coming? Yes! Now there's a team of heroes! There's a group of "baseball" cards I'd like to see!

Closing
Prayer:
What a host of heroes enrich our lives. Help us to know and learn from the glorious people who speak through the Bible. Touch us as you have touched them. Amen.

Materials:
A dozen or so contemporary baseball cards. For added effect, the leader might design a couple of cards featuring people from the Old Testament to use when these individuals are mentioned in the "Leader Message." These pictures can be clipped from discarded Sunday school materials and pasted over regular cards. The personalities cited by the leader can vary widely and might stress certain individuals whose stories relate to the regular sermon of the day. The list in the message is made intentionally long to show the leader the possibilities. As written, the recitation of so many names may make the children restless, so the leader should be judicious in adjusting the length to suit the audience. As a variation, a single personality might be selected and that individual's story told in depth.

Scripture
References:
Will vary with personalities chosen, but the following may prove helpful: Noah—Genesis 6—9; Joseph and the many-colored coat—Genesis 37; Ruth—book of Ruth; Hannah—1 Samuel 2:18–21; Daniel in the lion's den—Daniel 6; David and Goliath—1 Samuel 17; John 14:1–7.

The Way

**Motivation/
Activity:**

The leader is not present, but the children are asked by another to come forward. As soon as the children are settled, the leader appears at the opposite end of the sanctuary. The leader is intently studying a hand-held compass. The leader wanders about consulting the compass and trying to get his/her bearings. The children observe all this with a probable mixture of delight and curiosity. The leader eventually joins the children in the traditional sermon location, but only after reaching that point by a very indirect route. On arrival the leader holds the compass out for the children to examine. If none of the children names it, the leader identifies the object as a compass.

**Guided
Discussion:**

Why do you suppose I had so much trouble finding my way today? (You were lost. Couldn't read the compass. Didn't listen when we called you. Didn't look up.) How do we use a compass? What is it good for? (To find places. To keep us from getting lost. Know the directions.)

Leader Message: One reason I had trouble with this compass is that, at first, I was holding it upside down. Believe me, everything looked strange when the directions were backward. According to my upside-down compass, you were supposed to be over there (points to opposite end of sanctuary) and the organ was over there (points to position opposite actual location of organ). It was confusing and, for a time, I was what we call disoriented. I didn't know where I was or where other things were. I couldn't figure out where I fit in or how to get from one place to another. I was lost, and because I didn't know how to use the compass or how to read it, I got more and more lost. But when I used the compass properly, everything became much clearer. I was able to find my way. Jesus said, "I am the way," and his teachings in the Bible form a sort of compass to help us understand where we are and where we are going. We study the Bible so that we can make better use of it as a tool and a guide in our lives. The Bible is our special compass and we must all learn to read and use it as God intended.

Closing Prayer: God, you have shown us the Way. Help us to use the Bible as a compass that leads us toward you. Guide our steps and strengthen us in our journey as we continually seek you. Amen.

Materials: A hand-held compass. One with a large, high-contrast dial that can be comfortably worn on a lead around the neck will be most useful and will eliminate the possibility of its being accidentally dropped. A pocket Bible might be displayed by the leader as he/she draws parallels between the compass and the Bible. A sermon of this sort might be particularly effective on a day when children are given Bibles.

Scripture
Reference: John 14:1–7

Love Letters

Motivation: The leader displays a mailbox.

Activity: The leader invites the children to think about what sorts of things might be inside.

Guided
Discussion: What might we find in this mailbox? (Bills. Letters. Packages. Advertisements. Magazines. Newspapers.) Where do they come from? (Various answers.) Can you remember the last thing you got in the mail? (Various answers.)

Leader
Message: It's fun and exciting to open the mailbox. Often we find both good news and bad news, but that doesn't seem to stop us from wanting to look inside. Inside this mailbox is some wonderful, exciting, and special news. Inside is some very, very

good news about our lives and about the world we live in. (Reaches inside and pulls out a Bible.) This Bible contains good news for each and every one of us. And, in fact, parts of the Bible are letters written by Saint Paul, a special Christian and one of Christ's disciples. In Paul's letters we find instructions on how to establish and maintain the church and how to live a Christian life. They are important letters filled with advice, instruction, and, most important, love. Together with the rest of what we call the New Testament, Paul's letters form a special message of love and good news.

Closing
Prayer: We thank you, O God, for communicating with us. Help us to open the Bible with a sense of anticipation, knowing that, as we read, we will be touched by the message of your love and by the power of your spirit. Amen.

Materials: A mailbox, preferably of the style shown in the illustration, and a Bible

Scripture
References: Any of Paul's letters, especially 1 Corinthians 12, Galatians 6, Ephesians 4:1–7, or Colossians 3:12–17.

Something's Afoot

Motivation: The children are asked to stand in a circle or a row.

Activity: The leader produces a rag and proceeds to wipe the shoes of each child.

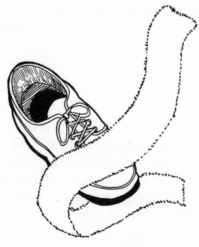

Guided
Discussion: How did you feel when I cleaned your shoes? (It tickled. Felt funny. Surprised. Embarrassed.) Did you expect me to do it? (No.)

Leader
Message: Let's sit down and I'll tell you a story about something Jesus once did. In Jesus' time only servants wiped the feet of others. It was considered a lowly job and

only the very poor or the very powerless were expected to do such things. One day, however, Jesus wanted to make a point, and he surprised all his friends by washing their feet. This made his friends uncomfortable, since they did not think it was right for their teacher and master—a person whom they admired—to do such a lowly task. But Jesus told them that if they wished to be great persons, they must first be willing to be servants. (The leader can close with a further interpretation of this parable, or he/she can proceed to the closing prayer.)

Closing
Prayer: Dear God, how you surprise us! Sometimes we become confused and think you love only powerful people. Instead, you have called us to serve one another even as you have served us. Continue to remind us of your truth. Amen.

Materials: A rag or cloth.

*Scripture
References:*   John 13:2–17; Philippians 2:5–8

Sound Advice

Motivation: The leader invites the children to listen carefully.

Activity: As the children listen, the leader gives a signal. From a point out of sight of the children comes the sound of someone hammering on a board. The leader signals again and the sound of someone knocking on a door is heard, again from a point out of sight of the children.

Guided
Discussion: Who can identify those sounds? (One was hammering. One was knocking.) Let's hear them again and see if you can tell me which is which. (Again the leader signals for each sound in turn, and the children respond with "hammering" or "knocking" as appropriate. Some children may say "Come in!" or "Who's there?" or ask who is

knocking, but these responses can be used to advantage.)

Leader
Message:

Although these two sounds are somewhat alike, those who listen carefully can tell the difference. The hammering may serve a purpose, but it is an unpleasant sound and we're glad when it stops. The knocking, however, fills us with interest. It makes us wonder (just as some of you did), "Who's there?" It makes us want to rush to the door and see who has come to visit. Jesus once said that he stood at our door and knocked. Let us all hope that we are listening carefully in this noisy world filled with hammering and other loud distractions so that when Jesus knocks, we are ready to answer the door.

Closing
Prayer:

O God, sharpen our hearing so we may identify your call from all the other noises that bombard our lives. Thank you for continuing to seek us—for continuing to knock—even when we fail to respond. Amen.

Materials:

None required, unless the leader decides to record or otherwise artificially produce the hammering and knocking sounds. The use of live volunteers, of course, requires timing and distinct cues. Rehearsal is recommended.

*Scripture
Reference:*

Revelation 3:20

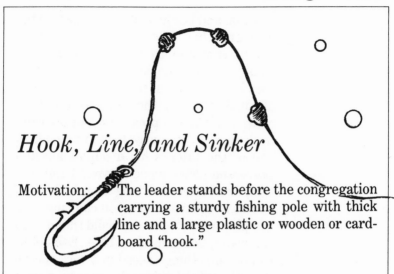

Hook, Line, and Sinker

Motivation: The leader stands before the congregation carrying a sturdy fishing pole with thick line and a large plastic or wooden or cardboard "hook."

Activity: The children are invited to pretend that they are fish quietly lying in a brook. The leader tries to encourage them to "take" the hook. Some will refuse, but others will probably grab hold. After a brief time, all materials are put aside.

Guided
Discussion: Where can people fish? (Lakes. Rivers. Streams. From boats. From shore.) Can you fish with anything besides a pole? (A boat. A net. A spear.)

Leader
Message: When Jesus first began to teach, he walked along the shores of a sea and watched workers fishing. The workers were not fishing for fun, but for food, and so they threw large nets into the sea and tried to catch as many fish as possible. Jesus invited some of these workers to

join him and become disciples. He told the workers that after joining him, they would continue to fish, but that they would fish for people. By that he meant that he would train them and teach them about God so that the disciples would become as skilled in preaching as they were in fishing. In this way Jesus was making use of the talents his disciples already possessed. Now some of you, I am certain, are better at fishing than I. Some of you have other talents: you can sing, you can play a sport, you can build things, you can swim, you can ride a bike. Each of us can do something special in a very special way. One of the things Jesus asks of us is that we use our talents to do God's work and invite others to discover God's love and God's plan for us.

Closing Prayer: Use us, dear God, as you used the fishers of old. Take our talents and direct them to your service. Let us serve as examples to others that they may know you through us. Amen.

Materials: A fishing pole, fashioned from a broom handle or bamboo rod, some soft white rope or yarn, and a hook-shaped piece of plastic, cardboard, or wood. Whatever substances are used for the line and hook, they should be of a nature so as not to injure tiny hands.

Scripture Reference: Luke 5:1–11

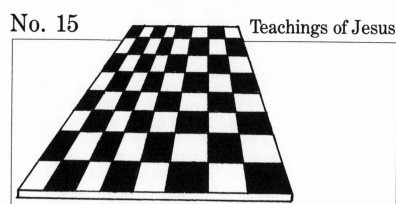

Check and Double-Check

Motivation:	The leader displays a metal checkerboard in a vertical manner so that both the children and the congregation can see it.
Activity:	The children are given magnetic checkers and invited to place them, one by one, on the board in positions that represent the beginning of a checkers match. One checker, however, is missing. When it is discovered that a piece is missing, the leader has the children look for it. It is eventually found and placed on the board. The board and checkers are put aside in preparation for discussion.
Guided Discussion:	Why was it necessary to find the missing checker? (Needed it to begin the game. Game could not be played without it. To make the sides even.)
Leader Message:	Although we had thirty-one other checkers, the set was not complete until we

found number thirty-two, the lost checker. The missing checker became important, and it was necessary to search for it. When we finally found it and put it with the others, I almost felt like cheering. I was glad to have it back. Jesus tells a story about something that was lost and then was found. A woman had ten silver coins, but one day she lost one of them. Rather than just forget about the missing coin, she lit a lamp and looked all over the house. She swept in the corners and looked under the beds until she finally found the missing coin. Then she called all her friends and neighbors together for a celebration. Jesus said that even though the woman was happy, her happiness could not compare with the happiness God feels when a lost sinner repents and returns. So we must always remember that if we turn from God—if we become the missing checker or the missing coin—no matter how far we stray, God will not abandon us and will rejoice when we return.

Closing Prayer:	We are so grateful, dear God, that you continue to seek us even when we are lost. Help us to remember that we are yours and that you will not abandon us. Find us now so we can live in the glory of your love. Amen.
Materials:	A metal checkerboard with magnetic checkers.
Scripture Reference:	Luke 15:8–10

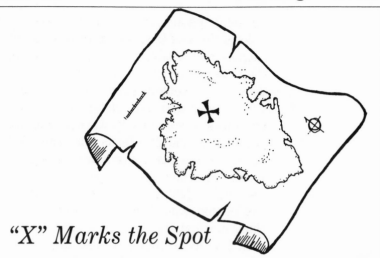

"X" Marks the Spot

Motivation: The leader displays a large map of an is-land, featuring palm trees, mountains, and other topographical features. A large *X* is visible on one portion of the map.

Activity: The leader selects a "starting point" on a side of the island opposite the *X* and asks two or three children to trace and de-scribe aloud the best route to get from various points to the *X*. After a few routes are explored, the map is put aside.

Guided
Discussion: What do you think the *X* stands for? (Place where treasure is buried; hiding place.) What sort of map is this? (A trea-sure map; pirate's map.) What do you think the treasure is? (Various answers, such as diamonds or gold.)

Leader
Message: We all think we know what a treasure is.

To some people, money is a treasure. Others think of jewels or precious metals such as gold or silver. Still others treasure their homes or other possessions. If we were more thoughtful, we might number our families and our friends among our treasures. Also, in many ways, our entire world is a treasure. Jesus once said that heaven is like a treasure hidden in a field. However, when this treasure is found, rather than just dig it up and take it away, the person who discovers it does something unusual. The person is so overcome with joy that rather than just dig up the treasure, the person leaves it in place, rushes home, sells everything he or she owns, and buys the entire field. It would be like finding a buried treasure on our island only to realize that the treasure is so valuable, so special, that it makes the island itself and everything on it a treasure too. The treasure of heaven, when discovered on earth, turns the entire world into a very special treasure.

Closing
Prayer:

Open our eyes and soften our hearts so we can see the treasures of our world. Expand our vision so that we may see the world itself and the world to come as wonderful treasures that you have planned for us. Amen.

Materials:

A hand-drawn treasure map with features as described above and a large X visible somewhere on the surface.

Scripture
Reference:

Matthew 13:44

The Neighborly Thing

Motivation: The leader displays a cardboard square on which have been glued a row of small house shapes.

Activity: Two or three children are chosen. The leader points to a house and asks, "If this was your house, who is your next door neighbor? (Pointing to adjacent houses.) Who lives here? And here?" After a few children have had turns, the cardboard is put aside.

Guided
Discussion: Who are our neighbors? (Various names. People who live next door. Next to us. Nearby. In our block/our neighborhood.)

Leader
Message: When Jesus told a man that he must love his neighbor as much as he loved himself, the man asked, "But who *is* my neighbor?" Jesus told him a story of a person who was attacked and beaten by robbers

as he walked down a road. The poor man was left for dead, lying in the dusty road. Several people passed by, including some who lived near him, but they all pretended not to see him and they didn't help him. Finally a stranger, a person from a distant land, who had never seen the injured man before, came along the road. The stranger immediately helped the injured man. Jesus emphasized that we should treat everyone like a neighbor, not just those who live nearby. We should love all others and take pity on them and help them whenever we can.

Closing
Prayer:

It is so much easier, God, to love people that we like. You have asked us to love all your people, even those who aren't lovable in our eyes. Strengthen our love so that we may share it freely with all your people. Amen.

Materials:

A square of cardboard on which have been mounted six or eight house shapes. Simple cutouts of the facades of single-story houses will suffice.

Scripture
Reference:

Luke 10:25–37

A Couple of Cups

Motivation: The leader displays cups of various shapes, sizes, and materials.

Activity: The children are asked to examine the cups and be prepared to tell how the cups are alike and how they are different.

Guided
Discussion: How are these cups different? (Various answers.) How are they alike? (All hold liquids. You drink from them. All are cup/bowl-shaped.)

Leader
Message: Like many of the tools we use, the cup is an extension of our own hands. (Leader puts hands together in a cup shape.) The cup resembles our cupped hands. When we take communion we take and eat bits

of bread and drink from a cup (leader pantomimes this action). The cup is an important part of communion, not only because it holds liquid, but also because it is an extension—a part—of each of us. (Leader again makes a cup shape with his/her hands.) We should put ourselves into communion and become part of it. Just as we put ourselves into and become part of prayer. (On saying this, the leader folds his/her cupped hands into a praying pose and leads the children in the closing prayer.)

Closing
Prayer:

God, we are continually amazed at the beauty of our bodies and the many things we can do. Help us to use our bodies as cups to receive the outpouring of your love and to see ourselves as part of your holy creation. Amen.

Materials:

Various cups (preferably nonbreakable) with and without handles. The hand gestures suggested in the "Leader Message" can be quite effective if coordinated with the narrative. A certain amount of rehearsal is suggested.

Scripture
Reference:

Matthew 26:26–28

Last But Not Least

Motivation: The leader appears before the children dressed in a jogging outfit and wearing a blue ribbon.

Activity: The leader invites the children to jog in place with him/her for a moment or to do warm-up exercises or to take a leisurely run around the sanctuary.

Group
Discussion: Do you race? Do you know anyone who races? What does this ribbon mean? (You're the winner. Won first place. Came in first. Best runner. Won the race.) What sort of ribbon would I get if I came in last? (Various colors. None. No prize for last.) What does it mean to be last? (Loser. Last one over the finish line. Didn't win.)

Leader Message:

We have formed an idea of what it means to be last as a result of our desire to win. Being first is important. We have come to think of first place as the best and most desirable place. But today I want you to think for a moment about a famous "last": the Last Supper. When we celebrate communion, as we are doing today, we are re-creating a special event in Jesus' life: his last meal among his friends. Certainly the first time they ate together was memorable, but not so memorable as this last supper. Jesus had much to say to his friends at the last supper, and much of what he said troubled them. He told them he was leaving for a time but not to lose faith because he would reappear and be with them forever. His friends were afraid; they thought they would be left behind; they thought they would be last. Jesus comforted them, however, and assured them that they could not yet follow where he was going, but that when their time came to join him, there would be places for all. Jesus asked only that his friends keep God's commandments, remain faithful, and remember him when they ate and drank. From that last request came our communion ceremony. When we eat and drink at communion, we remember Jesus and the Last Supper, and we promise to keep God's commandments. In return, we receive the gift of communion: God's promise that in the world to come there is no first or last, but there is a place for all who believe.

Closing
Prayer: Thank you, dear God, for the symbols that
           remind us of your love and of the impor-
           tant truth of Jesus. Remind each of us
           that, whether first or last, you have made
           a place for each of us. Amen.

Materials: A jogging outfit and a blue ribbon. The
           leader will naturally take into account the
           decorum of the sanctuary and the nature
           of the congregation in choosing an outfit
           and in selecting the intensity of the jog-
           ging activity.

Scripture
Reference: John 13—14

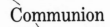

Sponge Plunge

Motivation: The leader displays several small, dry pieces of sponge and an aquarium or other container filled with water.

Activity: The children are invited to feel and handle the dry sponge pieces.

Guided
Discussion: How did the sponges feel? (Hard. Rough. Dry. Crusty.) Can we use sponges when they are like this? (No.) How can we make them softer and more useful? (Soak them in the water. Add water.) Let's place our sponges in the water. (Take a few moments to watch the effect of the sponges soaking up water and then cover the aquarium or place it to one side.)

Leader
Message: Today our congregation is sharing communion. Every now and then people find themselves getting stiff and rough and crusty just like our dry sponges. When people take communion they feel softer

and more useful to God. Communion changes us and helps us become fresher; it helps us renew our commitment to God and to the life God offers us.

Closing
Prayer:

Restore us, O God, to your way. Sometimes we are stiff and rough and crusty. We become frightened, insecure, and protective. Your love can make us open, responsive, and useful. Amen.

Materials:

Sponge pieces and an aquarium, or other transparent container, filled with water. A transparent, plastic fruit or vegetable crisper drawer from a refrigerator might be used, since it has the advantages of being accessible, lightweight, and non-breakable. Because any container filled with water will be bulky and difficult to move, it will be best if the water container can be placed on a secure rolling stand, or if the container can be put in a secure place and covered with a cloth when not in use. The leader should experiment with various sizes, types, and colors of sponges to find ones that yield dramatic results when placed in water. Certain "natural" sponges may prove effective, although they are not as colorful as processed sponges. Novelty sponges, such as expanding "dollar bills," and other such items could be used. A variety of colors among the sponge pieces can be effective.

Scripture
Reference: Mark 14:22–26

The Nose Knows

Motivation: The leader displays a container divided into two distinct compartments. One compartment contains baby powder and the other contains white flour.

Activity: The leader passes among the children and invites each to place one finger from the right hand and one finger from the left hand in the right and left compartments, respectively. (This process is easier to communicate by demonstration.) The children are asked to think about whether the substances in each compartment are the same or different.

Guided
Discussion: Are these white powders the same? (If the children say they are, invite them to smell each finger. If they have already discovered the aroma of the baby powder, they will probably report it in various forms. Discuss how the two powders differ in that one has a special aroma and the other doesn't. Identify one as flour and the other as baby powder. Pass around a small towel to wipe fingers.)

Leader	
Message:	Many things are known for their special smell or aroma; sometimes we refer to this as the essence of something. Bacon frying in the morning has a special essence; perfume has a pleasant essence. Think of the wonderful essence of a pie baking in the oven. (Children will probably say, *"Ymmmmm"* at this suggestion.) The essence of something cannot be seen, but it is special. Imagine the essence of flowers or the fresh, clean smell after a rainstorm. Certainly the essence of these things is important. The Bible suggests that a good Christian should be a kind of pleasant, refreshing, stimulating, sweet-smelling essence: an essence that sets the Christian apart and invites others to pay attention. Often others can learn about Christ by encountering a Christian who gives off an essence of love and caring.

Closing	
Prayer:	Praise be to you, O God, for the many ways we can know you. Make us sensitive to your essence. Amen.

| **Materials:** | A container with two distinct compartments and a small quantity of flour and baby powder. (The leader may want to caution very young children not to taste the powders.) A small towel should be provided to wipe hands. |

Scripture	
References:	2 Corinthians 2:14–17; Ephesians 5:1–2

Key Witness

Motivation: The leader displays a large ring of keys.

Activity: The children are invited to examine the keys as they are passed from child to child. On return to the leader, the keys are placed to one side.

Guided
Discussion: What do we do with keys? (Lock and unlock things. Open doors, cars, etc.)

Leader
Message: Most of us have seen courtroom scenes on television or in the movies. In a typical courtroom trial, people are allowed to present evidence by testifying. Testifying means telling the truth about something, telling what really happened. A person who testifies is called a witness. If a person's testimony is very important, that person is called a key witness. A key wit-

ness is a special witness because what he or she says can unlock the truth and help others to see the truth. In the Bible, John the Baptist was a key witness who foretold the coming of Christ and the meaning of Christ's appearance. God also calls on us to be witnesses—key witnesses—to help others unlock the truth of God's word.

Closing
Prayer:

God, we have seen and felt your love. Let us be like keys that unlock and open doors that others may enter and come to know you. Like a key witness, help us to live so clearly in your love that all who know us will see the truth of your spirit. Amen.

Materials:

A large ring of keys of various shapes, colors, styles, and sizes.

Scripture Reference:

Matthew 16:17

Meet Your Maker

Motivation: The leader displays two or three handcrafted items: for example, a wood carv-
ing, a weaving, a keyring.

Activity: The leader passes the items around, invit-
ing the children to handle and study each.

Guided
Discussion: Did you notice anything special about
these items? (Children may report color
or tactile sensations. Perhaps someone
will notice that they are handmade. If not,
the leader can draw attention to this.)
What's so special about something that is
made by hand? How does it differ from
something made by machine? (More ex-
pensive. Better quality. Prettier. Know
the person who made it. Special.)

Leader
Message: These handmade items are special to me
because whenever I look at them, I re-
member the person who made each thing.
(Taking an item, the leader describes the
person who made it. This procedure is
repeated for each item.) It makes things
special when you know the maker. That,
for me, is what makes the entire world

and the sun and the moon and all the stars so wonderful to me: because every time I see these things, I see the one who made them all. I know the maker of these things because I know God.

Closing
Prayer: O Creator and Maker of the world, how wonderful is your handiwork! Open our eyes that we may see your precious touch in beauty all around us. Amen.

Materials: Two or three handcrafted items. These can be well-fashioned items or less perfect crafts. The important thing is that each should have a "history" and call to mind a person whom the leader can honestly and enthusiastically describe to the children.

Scripture
Reference: Psalm 110:2

Today's Special

Motivation:	The leader displays a menu.
Activity:	The children are asked to examine the document and think about what they might order.
Guided Discussion:	What would you order from this menu? (Various answers, with an emphasis on the desserts, no doubt.)

Leader
Message: Have you ever wished that you could
            order everything on the menu and just
            have it all brought to your table in one
            huge, delicious bunch? Most of us, how-
            ever, must pay attention to our stomachs
            and our pocketbooks, and we end up or-
            dering just a few items. But there is an-
            other kind of menu from which we can
            have anything and everything, and that is
            the menu of God's love. On this special
            menu are some wonderful things: love,
            goodness, happiness, peace, families, chil-
            dren, and joy—to name a few. God shows
            us this wonderful menu and says, "All
            these are yours, all these and more, when
            you accept and follow God and Jesus."

Closing
Prayer: What an amazing and wonderful world
            you have spread before us. The goodness
            that surrounds us speaks of your love.
            Free us to select those things that allow
            us to live full lives in your world of love,
            light, and peace. Amen.

Materials: A colorful menu with lots of pictures.
            More than one may be provided if there
            are several children.

Scripture
Reference: Galatians 5:22, 25

Read the Label

Motivation: The leader displays a shopping bag or cart filled with various commercial soup cans, cartons, boxes, etc.

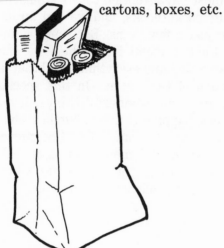

Activity: The leader invites the children to examine the labels on these items.

Guided
Discussion: Can anyone read any words on these labels? (Allow volunteers to read aloud. After a few have had an opportunity, the groceries are put aside.)

Leader
Message: The labels on packages contain a lot of information: they tell us what something is made of, how to cook it, how to open the package, and other useful information. If we read the entire label, we have a pretty good idea of what's inside and whether we

will like it or not. Unfortunately, labels are not always good. For example, when we try to label people and try to guess what's in their hearts or minds just by looking at the outside, we are being unfair. God teaches us that it's what's inside that counts. Outward appearances can be deceiving. I hope you will all remember not to label people just by their appearance. We need to talk to people and get to know them and find out more about them. If we do that, we have a special opportunity to talk to them about what's inside us and share with them our knowledge of God's love.

Closing
Prayer:

Forgive our temptation to label people like cans of soup. You show us over and over that within each person dwells a heart of beauty and a soul capable of Christian love. Give us eyes to see clearly the inner beauty of others. Amen.

Materials:

Four or five brightly colored and clearly labeled packages. Food items are probably best: cereal boxes, canned soups, etc. Contents could be emptied and packages resealed for ease of handling, but the children will probably be curious about why the packages are empty and this issue might distract from the sermon. The packages can be carried in a shopping bag, a shopping cart or basket, or a box.

Scripture
Reference: Psalm 51:6a

Handle with Care

Motivation:	The leader displays a large canvas or plastic bag and from it takes out several packages, each wrapped in plain brown wrapping paper and each sporting two or three brightly colored labels reading "Fragile," "Handle With Care," etc.
Activity:	The children are invited to handle the packages and pass them around.
Guided Discussion:	What do you think these packages contain? What's inside? (Various guesses. Some may guess fragile items, such as

glass. If no one mentions fragility, continue questioning, asking, "What do these labels say?") What does it mean when we say something is breakable or fragile? (It is easily broken. Will break if dropped.) Yes, these particular packages are empty, but if we were to send something fragile or breakable through the mail, these labels would be good reminders to those handling the packages to be careful with them. (The packages are put aside.)

Leader
Message:

The world is filled with fragile things: eggs, spiderwebs, light bulbs, drinking glasses, snowflakes. If such things are treated roughly or knocked about, they will surely break. Sometimes people can be fragile when they are particularly sad or angry or tired. And sometimes people can break, or parts of them can break. You've heard of a broken heart or a broken promise. People can be bruised and hurt and injured by what we do or don't do, and we can be hurt by others even when they don't mean to hurt us. We are all fragile at times. We are all capable of hurting others and being hurt ourselves. But there is a strength that gives us shelter and helps us when we are hurt. There is a power and a special caring that handles us with care because we are each a very special package containing very special things and bound for a very special place. This power is the power and strength of God's love.

Closing
Prayer: Remind us, O God, that in your eyes we are all precious and loved. Make us sensitive to the precious and fragile nature of people around us. Help us to treat others with kindness. Amen.

Materials: Small empty boxes wrapped in plain brown paper perhaps bound with string. Colorful "Fragile" and "Handle With Care" stickers. It is recommended that the boxes be empty for ease in handling, but the leader may wish to place a few fragile objects (such as Christmas bulbs) in each, taking care to pack them carefully to prevent damage if the boxes are dropped. Placing objects in each box would eliminate having to make the rather distracting announcement that the boxes are empty and may also afford the opportunity to emphasize some special message (for example, using the presence of Christmas bulbs to emphasize a holiday message, or placing small fragile plants in each to emphasize spring or Easter). An extra step of opening one or two boxes and examining the contents might be added to the foregoing activity, discussion, or message. However, unless the boxes are to be opened, or some point made regarding their contents, it will probably be best to leave them empty lest a child accidentally break something and be made to suffer the accompanying embarrassment and remorse that younger children feel so keenly.

*Scripture
References:* Isaiah 40:11; Micah 6:8; Luke 10:27b

Remote Control

Motivation: The leader displays a small remote-controlled car.

Activity: As the leader gives commands, the car (operated by an unseen helper) "obeys." A few children may be invited to give commands as well. After a few demonstrations, the operator is revealed and the procedure explained. The operator departs with the car.

Guided
Discussion: What made the car turn and stop? (The person with the controls.) Did you really think the car was obeying me? (No. Knew it was a trick. Have one at home. Some children, however, may mention they've seen voice-command vehicles on TV or elsewhere.)

Leader
Message: Most of us knew there was something somewhere controlling the car besides just my voice. There was an unseen force operating a signal and making the car go

and stop. Sometimes people are controlled by unseen signals. They come and go and do or don't do things in a way that makes us suspect they are receiving signals from an unseen source. Of course, people and toy cars are not the same. The car didn't have any choice when its controls were moved. It had to go left or right or stop when the controls said so. But people have a choice. They get a signal from God that says, "Do good," and they may receive signals from other sources that say, "Do bad." Every day we are faced with choices between good and evil. The good news is that God wants us to choose to do good and that, to help us, God sends us a powerful signal. The signal is God's special and powerful love guiding us to do the right thing.

Closing
Prayer:

God, sharpen our ears, brighten our eyes, and warm our hearts so that we can receive your signals and rejoice at your message. Amen.

Materials:

A small remote-controlled car or other remote-controlled toy, an operating switch, and a willing assistant. Depending on the toy and the surface to be used, a special board may have to be provided to ensure traction. A rehearsal and test of the procedure are essential.

Scripture
Reference:

Genesis 12:1–3

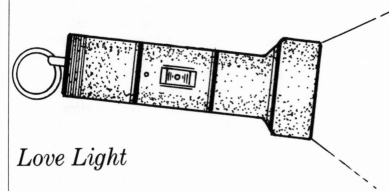

Love Light

Motivation: The leader displays two flashlights. Each is a different color, but both are the same general size and shape.

Activity: The children are invited to watch closely. The leader switches on both flashlights and points them so the children can clearly see each beam.

Guided
Discussion: Which of these flashlights works better? (Children name the color of the flashlight with the brighter beam.) Why do you think this one is brighter? (Has better batteries. Newer batteries.)

Leader
Message: Flashlights get their power from batteries. So do radios and cars and trucks. As people, we run on other kinds of things: we need food and water and sleep.

If we don't get these things, we don't work well. We get run down and, often, we get sick. Food and water and sleep are as important as batteries when it comes to keeping our human lights glowing. But there is one more thing we all need: we need love. A flashlight can get along quite well without love, but people need love. Loving others and being loved are the ways we charge our batteries. God sets a special example where love is concerned: God loves us all, and each week God invites us here to the church to recharge our Christian energy.

Closing
Prayer:

God, there are days when our light grows dim. Enliven us with your love and charge us to spread the light of that love to those who need us. Brighten our light that others may see your love in us. Amen.

Materials:

Two flashlights of similar shape and size, but of contrasting colors. One flashlight should have weak batteries and the other should have new, strong batteries so that the difference in light will be apparent. The leader should experiment in the sanctuary under light conditions similar to those that will exist at sermon time to ensure that the proper effect is achieved. If possible, sanctuary lights might be dimmed during the sermon for added emphasis.

Scripture
References:

John 1:1–9; 1 John 4:19, 21; John 8:12

A Good Clip

Motivation: The leader displays a large, brightly colored box.

Activity: The leader invites the children to listen closely as the box is tilted to and fro. (Unknown to the children, a small paper clip has been placed inside the box.)

Guided Discussion: What do you think this box contains? What's inside? (Various guesses.) Shall I give you some clues? This is something without which no office would be complete. Schools use this item too, and you probably have at least one at home. It is something most of us see or use often. It is small, but for many purposes it is the only thing that is suitable. (Various guesses.)

Leader Message: (The leader opens the box to reveal a paper clip.) This small piece of wire is important. We use it for many things, but mainly we use it to hold things together. For example, we can clip several papers together (demonstrates) and, when our clip is in place, it's hardly noticeable. In fact, I imagine a lot of people take the paper clip for granted, especially people who have lots and lots of paper clips. But suppose you couldn't find a paper clip when you needed one. How you would long for one! You know, many people are searching for something to hold their lives together the way a paper clip holds papers together. These people look and look for that special something, and sometimes their search brings them to a church such as ours. These visitors enter quietly. They look and they listen and they marvel at how our congregation works together and holds together, and they long to be part of all that. But sometimes such visitors are unable to understand the things that unite us, or they feel that we are so united we don't have room or time for new people; so they go away and look elsewhere. When visitors go away unfulfilled, we have failed them partly because we have forgotten to share the wonderful thing that holds us together: God's love. For us God's love seems such a wonderful truth that we don't always think about it or share it with others. Like the paper clip, we take God's love for granted, and we forget how special that love is. In the future let's all try to remember to share our beliefs and our faith with others so that they, too, can understand and join us in our special togetherness.

Closing
Prayer:

God, your love binds us together. We praise you for your love in our lives and for

the fact that this love makes us one people. Make us givers, as well as receivers,
of your binding love. Amen.

Materials: A large, brightly colored box and a small
paper clip. Some papers will be needed to
demonstrate the use of the paper clip.

Scripture
References: 1 John 4:7–16; Colossians 1:17–18a

The Magic Penny

Motivation: The leader displays a well-worn penny.

Activity: The children are invited to think about all the places this penny might have been.

Guided
Discussion: I have this penny just now, but where might it have been before I got it? How might it have been used? (Kept in the bank. Spent at the grocery store. Various other answers.) How might I spend this penny? (For candy. On a movie. Other answers.)

Leader
Message: In a way, this is a magic penny. It has already been many places, but today I'm going to send it off on a special journey. When the collection plate comes to me today, I'm going to put this penny—and some other money—into the plate and send it all the way to (leader could emphasize a special project being supported by today's offering). So, we can soon say good-bye to this penny, but we needn't be sad. This penny is going on a great adventure and it will see many things. It will

see unhappy things, such as (poverty, disease, or other applicable situations), but it will also see happy things (people being fed and clothed, people building shelters and churches, etc.). Not only will it see happy things, but it will also help make happy things happen! Now, you may think that this little penny has a big job ahead of it (fighting disease and poverty, performing other tasks), but remember, it won't be alone. If you turn and look at the congregation, you will see people holding up pennies and nickels and dimes and quarters and dollar bills and checks and pledge envelopes—all getting ready to join our magic penny on its splendid journey to help others. Isn't that a wonderful sight!

Closing
Prayer:
What wonderful things you can do with our lives, O God. Just as our money travels all over the world helping other people, so your love and support span the globe. Take us, our work, and our money. We dedicate ourselves to your service. Amen.

Materials:
A well-worn penny plus the cooperation of the congregation. The latter is probably best obtained by placing a request in the bulletin or program asking members of the congregation to hold a bit of change or a dollar or two aloft on cue during the children's sermon.

Scripture
Reference: 2 Corinthians 9:6–15

Out of the Groove

Motivation:
The leader displays two long-playing (33⅓ rpm) records. One is shiny and new; the other is badly scuffed, scratched, and warped.

Activity:
The children are invited to examine the damaged record and suggest what might have caused the record to become ruined.

Guided
Discussion:
What do you think damaged this record? (It got too hot or too cold. Someone left it in the sun. Someone didn't take care of it. Someone sat on it. Didn't play it right.) How can we keep records from becoming scratched or warped? (Take care of them. Keep them out of extreme temperatures. Be careful with them. Keep them in the protective paper cover. Use them correctly. Care for them.)

Leader
Message:
A record is a delicate thing. If it is not properly cared for, it can easily become damaged. You know, many people have

thought about what the human soul looks like. I like to think of the soul as a sort of record. As we live, we add lines and grooves to our soul, something like the lines on a record. When the soul is cared for, it stays smooth and beautiful and it records and plays back the beautiful music of joy and peace. But when the soul becomes heated in anger, or frozen with bitterness, or scratched by conflict, it warps and the music sounds terrible. The soul is not *exactly* like a record, however, because—even if it is scratched and warped —the human soul can be saved; the human soul is recyclable. The soul can become smooth and beautiful again and its music can fill the world with joy and peace. Join with me now in that special experience that mends the human soul: let us pray . . .

Closing
Prayer: Dear God, restore us with your love. We have damaged our souls through selfishness. Your love can make us like new again. Thank you for the new life available to each of us through our dedication to your word. Amen.

Materials: Two records: one undamaged and the other badly scratched, scuffed, and warped. Suitable LPs can be economically obtained from a local thrift store or a used-merchandise store.

Scripture
References: Ephesians 4:25–32; Luke 5:17–26; Revelation 21:5

The Year of Our Lord

Motivation: The leader produces a calendar showing December of the year just ended and January of the next year. In front of each year the leader has written A.D. in large letters so that, for example, "December 1987" reads "December A.D. 1987."

Activity/
Guided
Discussion: The leader invites the children to tell what the A.D. means. (Answers will vary. Some may suggest "after Christ" or "in the year of our Lord," but others will have less informed guesses.)

Leader
Message: The letters A.D. stand for the Latin phrase *anno Domini*, which means "in the

year of our Lord." Another pair of letters, B.C., stands for "before Christ." The years of our history are divided into two main parts: The B.C. years—before Christ—are the years before Jesus was born, and the A.D. years—the years of our Lord—are the years after Jesus was born. In other words, there was a point in time before Jesus came into the world and there is the time since his appearance. For nearly two thousand years Christians have been celebrating each year of our Lord. This celebration is especially joyous at the beginning of each new year. Each new year means a new start, a chance to begin again. When God sent Jesus to live and teach in this world, God offered all people a new beginning. Just as the coming of each new year fills us with hope for the future, the reality of Jesus' birth and his presence in our lives makes every year *anno Domini*—truly the year of our Lord.

Closing Prayer:	How amazing is your love, Lord. Like the year, we can become new again. Help us to shed the scars and sadness of the past and live in your love as new people. Amen.
Materials:	Calendar pages: one for December of the outgoing year and one for January of the new year. The letters A.D. are written in front of the year on each calendar page (for example, A.D. 1987 and A.D. 1988).
Scripture References:	Mark 7:31–37; Revelation 21:5

Heart, Take Wing

Motivation: The leader displays a tightly closed,
                frosted plastic container inside which a
                red heart-shaped balloon is dimly visible.

Activity: The leader invites the children to examine
                the contents of the container without
                opening it as it is passed from child to
                child.

Guided
Discussion: What could you see inside? (A heart.
                Heart balloon. Heart shape. Valentine.)
                Could you see it clearly? (No. It was
                blurred. Container not clear.) The leader
                holds the container before him/her and
                begins the "Leader Message."

Leader Message:	This is the season of hearts; we see them everywhere. Hearts on windows, in stores, and on colorful cards. And yet much of the time, even on Valentine's Day, we hide our true hearts and our true feelings so that others cannot see them clearly. We lock our true hearts away inside little containers and force people to try and guess our feelings. We close our hearts to others. And yet—not only on Valentine's Day, but year-round—God tells us to open our hearts to others. To love people openly and freely. That is the message of Valentine's Day and it is God's message to each of us: to open our hearts and share our love with all the world. (So saying, the leader opens the container and the heart balloon—which is filled with helium—floats up and away.)
Closing Prayer:	Help us, dear God, to share our hearts. Grant that we may be able freely to show your love to others. Help us to love others as you have loved us. Amen.
Materials:	A frosted plastic container with a lid that seals tightly but can be easily opened. A heart-shaped, helium-filled balloon. Because a helium-filled balloon that is allowed to sit dormant for some time loses its buoyancy, it will be best if the balloon is not placed in the container too far in advance of the event. A few rehearsals are recommended.
Scripture References:	1 John 4:4–21; 1 Corinthians 13:8–13

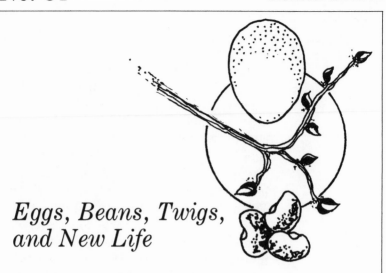

Eggs, Beans, Twigs, and New Life

Motivation: The leader displays an egg, some dry beans, and a dormant twig with buds.

Activity: The children are invited to examine these objects and think about what each represents.

Guided Discussion: What might happen if this egg is hatched? (A new chick or bird or other animal would be born.) When these beans are planted, what will grow? (A plant. More beans. A flower. A beanstalk.) When spring comes, what will happen to the little buds on this branch? (They will become leaves. Grow into blossoms.) Are these things living or dead? (Living.)

Leader Message: During the lenten season we talk a great deal about Jesus and about life and death.

The fact that such things as eggs, beans, and twigs can appear dead and yet come to life is a reminder that when we follow Jesus, a new life awaits us all. The egg is a promise of a new chick, the beans are a promise of growing plants, and—at the touch of spring—this twig will fulfill the promise of fresh green leaves. The promise of new life is an important part of the lenten message. During Lent we need to take a close look at ourselves and ask: Are we living new lives? Are we living lives made fuller and richer by the knowledge of Jesus?

Closing
Prayer: Jesus, our lives are made full by your promise of new life. Strengthen our faith that we might see the fulfillment of your promise in the world around us. Help us to see beyond the cross to recognize the value of your victorious life. Amen.

Materials: An egg (hard-boiled for safety's sake), a handful of beans, and a twig with highly visible buds. The leader should be prepared for well-informed comments from children that a hard-boiled egg or one removed from the nest, as well as a plucked twig, are not likely to yield life. If such comments are anticipated, other items might be substituted. The safest route is to use seeds exclusively (i.e., beans along with other interesting seeds common to the local area).

Scripture
References: John 17; 1 Corinthians 15:35–38

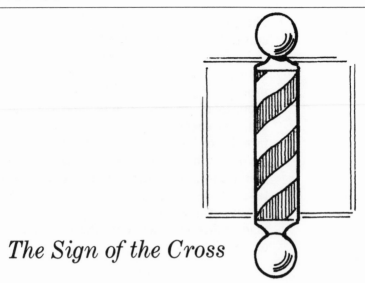

The Sign of the Cross

Motivation: The leader displays colorful pictures of
              various trademarks or signs that the chil-
              dren are likely to recognize (for example,
              a barber pole, a fish or shoe silhouette, a
              popular commercial trademark). The
              leader asks the children to tell what sort
              of shop would have each sign on display
              outside. (Various answers.)

Activity: The leader puts the pictures aside and
              produces two long rectangles (one slightly
              longer than the other) that have been cut
              from cardboard or wood. The leader in-
              vites the children to use these materials to
              design a symbol or a sign that would be
              placed outside the church. (A cross may
              be produced, although other shapes are
              possible. If the children do not produce a
              cross in a short time, the leader should
              make one, commenting that the other

shapes are interesting, and ask the children if they recognize the familiar cross shape.)

Guided
Discussion:

What does the cross mean to you? What does it stand for? (The place where Jesus was crucified. Our church. Christianity. Christians.) What do you think about when you see the cross? (Jesus. His death. His sacrifice. His resurrection. Our church. Easter.)

(Note: Such complex terms as crucifixion, resurrection, and sacrifice may or may not be volunteered by the children. The purpose of this activity is not to discuss in depth the meaning of such concepts, or even to have the children offer such words, but rather to focus on the cross as an important Christian symbol or sign.)

Leader
Message:

Did you notice how easy it was to make a cross? Sometimes a simple shape can get lost among the fancy, blinking neon signs and other colorful symbols and shapes of our everyday world. Today is Easter Sunday, a time when the cross is very special. Let's all try to remember to look to the cross and to recognize it as a very special Christian sign.

Closing
Prayer:

O Risen Christ, what a wonderful sign you offer in our lives. To us the empty cross is an ever-present reminder of your victory over death and of our hope for forgiveness of our sins. Help us to live as you intended. Amen.

Materials: Photographs or drawings or cutouts depicting various recognizable commercial symbols such as those mentioned above. Actual trademarks or logos that the children would recognize might be used. An alternative would be to display a picture showing several business signs along a major street. The materials to construct the cross could be colored pasteboard or cardboard or pieces of wood (free from splinters). If the leader wants the congregation to see the construction process, a flannel board mounted on an easel might be used with the cross pieces made of appropriate cloth. Cross pieces and background should be of contrasting colors. A kindergarten, primary, or preschool teacher in the congregation would be a good resource for advice in constructing flannel board materials.

Scripture Reference: Matthew 28:1–8

Shout It Out

Motivation: The leader begins addressing the children
                   by whispering such instructions as "Sit
                   down, please" or "Move closer together,
                   please."

Activity: The children listen intently.

Guided
Discussion: (Still in a soft voice.) You all impress me
                   as children with good strong voices and
                   yet I notice that you all speak very quietly
                   in church. Why do you speak so softly
                   here? (Many interesting responses will be
                   given, including such answers as "So as
                   not to disturb the preachers.") Well, those
                   are good reasons, but let's consider today
                   a special occasion. How would you speak if
                   you had some exciting news to share?
                   (Louder. Would shout.)

Leader
Message: (In a louder voice.) Well, I'm here to tell
                   you that Easter is a shouting event! Jesus
                   Christ lives and I think that's exciting! So,
                   for today, let's shout out the good news

that "Christ is risen!" and we will ask the congregation to respond "Christ is risen indeed!" Ready? (The leader may wish to repeat the instructions. The leader directs the children and the congregation in turn. This exchange may have to be repeated two or three times before the children really do shout.) Thank you, children. Some events are so exciting and they are such good news that we really must shout about them. Easter is such an event. But it is also a time for quiet thought and prayer; let us all pray together . . .

Closing Prayer: (In a mild voice.) O God, you hear us when we whisper and when we shout. We praise you for loving us so much. Help us to use our voices to further your word and your holy work. Amen.

Materials: None. The cooperation of the children and the congregation is essential. The latter can be facilitated by announcing the activity in the bulletin, or order of worship, beforehand. This is a unique, and potentially volatile, activity that the leader may be hesitant to attempt. It is strongly suggested that the sermon begin and end on a quiet note. This will have a calming effect on the children while still allowing them to thrill themselves and the congregation by vigorously shouting aloud the news of Christ's glorious victory.

Scripture References: John 20:1–8; Psalm 100

"M" Is for Mary

Motivation: The leader displays a large letter *M*.

Activity: The leader invites the children to name the letter and think of words that begin with the *M* sound.

Guided
Discussion: What do you think this *M* stands for? (Various words.) Yes, those are good words, but this is a capital *M*, so it must stand for the name of something or someone. (Leader can, if necessary, give the following series of hints to aid the children.) What month is this? (May.) Could this *M* stand for May? (Yes.) What special holidays do we celebrate in May? (Various answers are possible, but the major holidays are Mother's Day, Memorial Day, and May Day. The leader may have to give assistance in identifying these days.)

Leader
Message: This *M* actually stands for four things that begin with the *M* sound: first the month of

May and then the two holidays we celebrate in May: Mother's Day and May Day. And last, but certainly not least, this *M* stands for a woman from the Bible who knew the joys of motherhood and rejoiced at the coming of spring. Her name is Mary; *M* is for Mary, the mother of Jesus. As we celebrate May and its holidays, I hope we will think of Mary and of the importance of motherhood and of the special promise of life that spring brings each year.

Closing
Prayer:

Dear God of May and mothers, you guide our lives. As Mary loved her son, so we love you and him. We praise you for the love of mothers and for the newness of spring. Amen.

Materials:

A large *M* (capital letter, not lower case). The letter can be cut out of construction paper, although a sturdier one of cardboard or pasteboard would be more effective. A three-dimensional letter of wood or other material might be used. The letter should be large enough to focus the children's attention, but not so large as to encumber the leader as he/she works with the children.

Scripture
Reference:

Luke 1:30–33

Balloon Zoom

Motivation: The leader displays two or three unin-
              flated balloons. The children are invited to
              tell how balloons are used. (Answers will
              vary, including for parties, on parade
              floats, for transportation, as decorations,
              for playing.)

Activity: The leader exclaims that balloons cer-
              tainly seem to be exciting things, and as
              the children watch closely, the leader
              holds the balloons up at arm's length and
              drops them. The balloons fall limply to the
              floor and (probably amid some excite-
              ment) they are all retrieved and returned
              to the leader.

Guided
Discussion: I don't understand. These balloons that
              you all seem to think are so wonderful
              don't seem special to me. They just

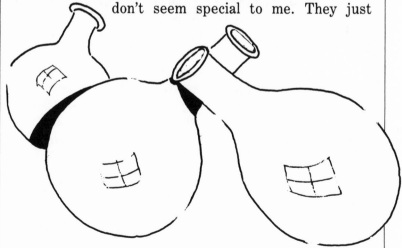

plopped down. What's wrong? (They need air. Helium. Got to fill them up. Blow them up. Put air in them.) Oh, I see. Well, I'm a little busy right now. I'll ask the members of the choir to blow these up later. (A choir member comes forward to collect the balloons; unknown to the children *all* choir members have balloons.)

Leader
Message:

Today I want to invite each of you to be filled with the spirit of God. I want to talk to you about Pentecost. Today we celebrate Pentecost, a time when the disciples of Jesus were greatly changed through an encounter with the Holy Spirit. Before the Holy Spirit filled them up, the disciples were limp and lifeless, like those empty balloons. But the Holy Spirit filled them with joy and grace. (On this signal, each choir member inflates a balloon. This action, visible to the children, should cause quite a stir. The leader should wait for the excitement to ebb a bit before continuing.) And when they were filled with the Holy Spirit, they were so overcome with excitement and energy that they rushed about spreading the good news to everyone. (All balloons are released. The children will undoubtedly react with glee.) Now that, my young friends, was something like the effect the Holy Spirit had on the disciples!

Closing
Prayer:

How exciting you can make our lives, dear God. Fill us with your spirit that we may soar to new heights of love and service. Amen.

Materials: Several colorful balloons. It will be best to get fairly pliable, round (as opposed to oblong) balloons and to prestretch them so that they will inflate more readily. This orchestrated excitement may seem a bit too rowdy for some sanctuaries. The leader needs to modify the format accordingly. Perhaps a single balloon will suffice. The purpose of the activity is to thrill the children and give them some sense of the rush of joy that must have characterized the disciples' encounter with the Holy Spirit. For an even more dramatic effect, the choir might—immediately after launching the balloons—erupt into a chorus of hallelujah. Members of the congregation might also inflate and release balloons, especially those members in the balcony. As a final note, it will be a good idea to check with the church custodian ahead of time to determine if stray balloons might pose a threat to heating or ventilation systems or to organ pipes. Be aware of the danger that errant balloons may become lodged in inaccessible spots, such as chandeliers. Also, it will be helpful if the leader and others volunteer to collect the balloons after the service. In general, when such a unique event is planned, the best rule of thumb is to check with all concerned parties well in advance of the performance to ensure consent and cooperation.

Scripture
Reference: Acts 2:1–13

In God We Trust

Motivation: The leader displays several coins and pa-
               per money of various denominations (all
               U.S. currency).

Activity: The children are invited to look closely at
               the pictures and words on the coins and
               bills.

Guided
Discussion: Based on the words and pictures you see
               on this money, what do you think people
               seeing it for the first time will think about
               our nation? (The leader may have to
               prompt for answers at first; for example,
               directing the children's attention to the
               back of a one dollar bill and saying, "What
               do you see here? [An eagle.] Do Amer-
               icans think the eagle is important?" [Yes.]
               Various answers should be expected: We

have great presidents. We believe in liberty. We have big buildings. We like the colors green and silver. We like eagles. Our country is called the United States. We trust in God.)

Leader
Message: Did you notice that on each coin and on each bit of paper money the four words "In God We Trust" are printed? The men and women who worked to create our nation felt that God should be at the center of American life. When we pledge allegiance to our flag, we say, "One nation under God." One of our favorite patriotic songs, "America, the Beautiful," praises God for shedding grace on our nation. (Ideally, the choir might have just finished singing this hymn.) And yet, as convinced as we Americans are that God is important, we have chosen to establish a nation in which each person is free to worship in his or her own way. This great freedom is called freedom of religion, and it makes this nation a special place in which to live. As we assemble each week to worship, let us remember those people who founded our nation, who put their trust in God, and who had the wisdom and courage to provide for freedom of religion.

Closing
Prayer: We praise you, our God, for the wisdom of those men and women who established

our country. We thank you for guiding them to ensure our freedom to worship you. Make us aware of this great gift and strengthen our will to preserve it. Amen.

Materials: Various coins (i.e., penny, nickel, dime, quarter, half-dollar, silver dollar) and assorted paper money (dollar bill, five-dollar bill, etc.). For ease of handling, coins and paper money might be mounted on a piece of cardboard. Coins could be laminated into a clear plastic sheet so that both sides are visible. The words "In God We Trust" are printed on the face of U.S. coins and on the reverse side of U.S. paper money.

Scripture Reference: Psalm 33:12

Run It Up the Flagpole

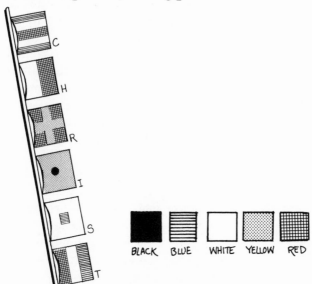

BLACK BLUE WHITE YELLOW RED

Motivation: The leader displays a long pole to which six colorful signal flags have been affixed.

Activity: The leader announces that these are signal flags used on ships to send messages, such as an S.O.S., a call for help. The children are invited to examine the flags and consider what sort of messages they might want to send from one ship to another.

Guided Discussion: What kind of message might you send to another ship? (Hello. Help, we're sinking! Various other answers.) What do you think these flags spell out? (Various guesses.)

Leader Message:	Those are all good guesses. The message of these flags is a message that people nearly two thousand years ago were longing to see. These flags spell Christ (point to each and spell C-h-r-i-s-t). Nearly two thousand years ago people waited and watched for the Christ whose coming had been predicted. And when at last Jesus, the Christ, appeared, it was as if a cry for help—an S.O.S.—had been answered. Even now, when we feel lost or discouraged, we seek the one represented by these colorful flags. And whether we say it aloud, or whisper it in a prayer, or read it or write it, or see it displayed on colorful flags flowing in an ocean breeze, it is a wonderful name: Christ Jesus; Jesus Christ; our Lord and Savior.
Closing Prayer:	Open our eyes, dear God, that we may see the signs of your love all around us. Give us the courage to unfurl our flags of faith and display your truth and love so that others will honor you in the lives we live. Amen.
Materials:	A pole from six to ten feet in length. Six square "flags" made of brightly colored construction paper or pasteboard or stiffened cloth. Flags are to be displayed in the order shown in the illustration. The color key is: lined sections are blue; crosshatched sections are red; dotted sections are yellow; black and white are as shown.
Scripture *Reference:*	Matthew 5:14–16

In the Beginning

Motivation: The leader displays a drawing showing the sun at its zenith with the remainder of the picture divided equally into darkness and light (see illustration).

Activity: The children are invited to study this picture and be prepared to describe what they see.

Guided
Discussion: What do you see here? (The sun. Daytime and nighttime.)

Leader
Message: This picture represents the idea of the beginning of autumn. On a certain day in September, daytime and nighttime are the same length; there are just as many hours of daylight as there are of darkness. This event is called the autumnal equinox,

an event that signals the beginning of the autumn season. On this first day of autumn, so the scientists say, the sun appears to pause in the sky. The coming of autumn in this dramatic way always reminds me of the Old Testament description of the creation of the earth, how God divided the day from the night and how God placed the sun and moon and stars in the sky.

Each time we make a new discovery, we learn how well-planned and how wonderful things really are and that just makes me all the more certain that God has touched everything in our world. This autumn, rather than being sad because summer is ending and winter is on its way, I hope you'll all pause and think about how carefully God created this wonderful, amazing world.

Closing
Prayer:

How amazing, O God, is your world. We marvel at the beauty of your creation and at the passage of the seasons. Continue to work in our lives that we may reflect the glory of your world. We are drawn to your eternal light. Amen.

Materials:

A drawing similar to the one shown. The day portion could be white, yellow, or another "daylight" color, whereas the night portion could be black, dark blue, light gray, or a similar night color. The sun could be yellow.

Scripture
References:

Genesis 1:1–5; Psalm 8:3–4

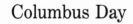

Serendipity

Motivation:	The leader displays a piece of pasteboard on which the word SERENDIPITY has been printed.
Activity:	The children are told the word and invited to consider what it might mean.
Guided Discussion:	What do you think the word serendipity means? (Various answers.)
Leader Message:	Those are good answers. This is not a word you hear often and so I really don't expect you to know its exact meaning. The word serendipity was first used in an old fairy tale about three princes who kept making happy discoveries by accident. For example, suppose every day you walked past a little store but never went inside. Then one day it was raining hard, so you popped inside to get dry and found a toy store filled with all sorts of delightful sights and sounds. You could say that you had an experience of serendipity; a sort of

happy accident. Each October we celebrate Columbus Day in honor of one of the first explorers to land in America. Christopher Columbus wasn't looking for America, he just sort of stumbled onto it in a happy accident: serendipity. Wouldn't it be nice if our lives were filled with happy accidents: discovering new lands, finding new treasures? As Christians, however, we know that many things do not happen by accident, and we know that not everything that happens will make us instantly happy. We know that sometimes life is difficult, but we also know that God has a plan for us. In short, no matter how bad things seem, we place our trust in God. We know that all things work together for good for those who love God. Serendipity is a wonderful word, but—as Christians—we have an even stronger and an even better word, one that I hope you and all the congregation use often: that word is (turn card over) FAITH.

Closing
Prayer: Dear God, we place our lives in your hands. You surprise us with the care you give us. Strengthen our faith so we may trust you more and be less afraid. Life can be difficult, but you have promised that wonderful things await us. Amen.

Materials: A piece of pasteboard with the word SERENDIPITY printed on one side and the word FAITH on the other.

*Scripture
Reference:*   1 John 5:1–5

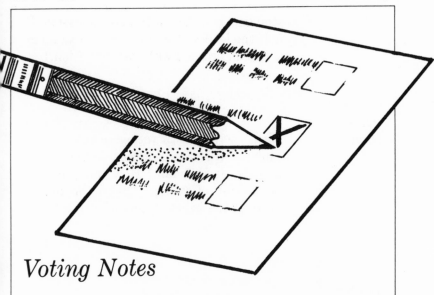

Voting Notes

Motivation: The leader unfolds a large sample ballot containing many choices of candidates and ballot issues.

Activity: The leader studies the ballot but does not let the children peek at it. The leader says something like: "I'm looking at the names of three candidates who are running for election. All of you who think the first one should be elected raise your hands. Good. How about the second one? Good. Does anyone want to vote for the third one? All right. Now, let's look at one of the questions to be decided on the ballot. I'm looking at a question that can be voted on yes or no. How many say yes? How many say no? (Sometime during this activity a child may interrupt and say, "Let us see" or "We can't see!" If so, the leader should stop and go on to the guided discussion. If not, the leader should finish the examples and then proceed with the discussion.)

Guided
Discussion:

What's wrong with voting this way? (We can't see the names/choices. You won't let us look. It isn't fair.) How can you do a better job of voting? (Read the paper. Look at the ballot. Know what the ballot says.)

Leader
Message:

Election time is coming up (or has just passed), and one of the main problems with some voters is that they go to vote without knowing enough about the candidates running for office or about the issues to be decided. They don't read the ballot and so, when they vote, they are just sort of guessing. The ballot is a guide, and if we don't read it, we don't make good choices. Of course, besides making choices when we vote each November, each of us makes hundreds of choices every week. We choose to act in certain ways, to say certain things, to do things, or to leave things undone. And many times we make choices by just guessing, without any kind of plan or any guide about which choice is good or bad. To make good choices as a voter, we use the ballot as a guide. To make good choices in life, we have a guide too; we call it the

Bible (leader holds up Bible). The more
we read and study this valuable guide, the
more likely we are to make choices that
reflect the sort of life God intended us to
live.

Closing
Prayer: Thank you, God, for the freedom to
             choose. Guide our choices that we may do
             your will in our lives. Forgive us when we
             make choices that ignore your will. Amen.

Materials: A sample ballot and a Bible.

Scripture
Reference: Deuteronomy 30:19–20

Polite Delight

Motivation/
Activity:　　　The leader directs the children's attention
to two members of the choir or con-
gregation. The children are asked to listen
as the two speak the following dialogue:

    1: *(brusquely)* Give me that hymnal.
    2: This one?
    1: *(sharply)* Yes.
    2: All right. Here. (Hands hymnal to
       1.)
    1: *(coldly)* About time. (1 and 2 glare at
       each other and sit down abruptly.)

The leader now asks the children to watch
and listen again as the two actors repeat
their scene as follows:

    1: *(pleasantly)* May I have that hymnal
       please?
    2: This one?
    1: *(smiling)* Yes. (Receives the hymnal
       from 1.) Thank you.
    2: You're welcome. (1 and 2 sit down
       contentedly.)

Guided
Discussion:　　Did you notice any difference in the way
these people talked to each other the second time? (They were polite. Said please
and thank you and you're welcome. Didn't
fight or argue.)

Leader Message:	This month we celebrate Thanksgiving, a special holiday set aside to give thanks to God for all the wonderful treasures we enjoy. The giving of thanks and polite behavior, like saying, "Please" and "You're welcome," are things we do to show others that we care about their feelings. When we are polite we feel good and the people around us feel good too. Think what a wonderful world it would be if we spent the entire year—and all our lives—being polite and showing our thankfulness to God and to all people.
Closing Prayer:	O God, we are fragile and easily hurt. We also know that other people are sensitive to how we care for them. Help us to love one another. Help us to act in kindness. Amen.
Materials:	No materials are needed other than scripts for two volunteer actors and a hymnal to serve as a prop.
Scripture *References:*	Psalms 100:3–5; 103:1–5

Wrapped Attention

Motivation: The leader displays gift wrapping items: a
               bow, a length of ribbon or yarn, cello-
               phane tape, wrapping paper, and a small
               empty box.

Activity: A few children are invited to demonstrate
               the procedure for wrapping a gift. This is
               best accomplished by handing the empty
               box to one child and asking, "What do you
               do first?" Once the paper is in place, the
               child can pass the package to another who
               can tape the edges. Thus the entire wrap-
               ping procedure can proceed from child to
               child. It will be best to show at first that
               the box is empty to eliminate the question
               "What's in here?" and attendant distrac-
               tions. If the leader is concerned about the
               child-to-child procedure, an option is to
               solicit verbal instructions from the chil-
               dren while the leader or another adult

does the actual wrapping. The process of this activity is much more important than the finished product. Once finished, the package is placed to one side.

Guided
Discussion:

Why do we wrap packages? (To hide what's inside. To make them pretty. To get ready for Christmas.)

Leader
Message:

One way we prepare for the coming Christmas season is to wrap several packages in bright paper and decorate them with bows and strings and ribbons. We also prepare by decorating our houses with colored lights and trimming trees with lights, tinsel, and other ornaments. We do many things to prepare for Christmas, and our preparations often begin around this time of year, a time we call Advent. Advent includes the four Sundays before Christmas, the day we celebrate Christ's birth. Advent means "the coming of Christ," and it is during Advent that Christians around the world look forward to the Christmas celebration. From now on until Christmas Eve and Christmas Day, our eyes will behold a rainbow of bright colors. The outsides of houses and packages and trees will glow in brilliant shades of red and green and gold and silver. But, as we look in wonder at all this dazzling color, we must remember that the real preparation for Christmas, the real Advent, takes place inside each of us as we think about Jesus and the joy the knowledge of his birth gives us.

Closing
Prayer:

God, as we make ready for the holidays, remind us of the importance of preparing our hearts. Let the joy and excitement of this season transform us so that we can truly appreciate and celebrate the promise of Christmas. Amen.

Materials:

A small empty box, large enough for the children to manipulate, but not so large as to be cumbersome when passed from child to child. Wrapping paper, premeasured to fit the box so that additional cutting or time-consuming folding is not necessary. String, ribbon, or yarn premeasured to the package. Cellophane tape on an easily manipulated roll. A ribbon that easily adheres, preferably self-adhesive.

Scripture
Reference:

Isaiah 40:3

A Watched Clock

Motivation: The leader displays a cuckoo clock.

Activity: The children are invited to look at the clock and be prepared to tell what they see.

Guided Discussion: What is this? (Various answers, including a clock, a cuckoo clock.) What's special about it? (The cuckoo comes out. A bird comes out. There's a bird/cuckoo inside. It strikes the hour. It's old.)

Leader Message: Yes, this is a special clock called a cuckoo clock. A tiny little bird—carved out of wood—has been placed inside, and when the clock reaches the hour, the cuckoo will come out and sing a song. It's almost time for the cuckoo to come out, just a few seconds now. Let's all sit quietly and wait and watch for the cuckoo. (The children, the leader, and the congregation all sit—silent and expectant—for a few seconds until the cuckoo emerges. The children may smile and giggle in anticipation.) My, wasn't that exciting waiting for the cuckoo to come out! The feeling of nervous excitement is called anticipation. It's the same feeling we get during this advent season as we look forward to the joyous coming of Christmas and the celebration of Christ's day of birth. Remember that feeling and treasure it as the joyous Christmas season approaches!

Closing
Prayer: What joy we find, O God, in anticipation. Thank you for your promises made truth in the birth of Jesus. Help us to use this time of Advent to prepare our hearts to receive your love. Amen.

Materials: A cuckoo clock that is firmly mounted on a stand or table. The leader will want to rehearse with the clock a few times to ensure timing. A wait of around a minute and a half should give the leader time to complete the activity and guided discussion and still leave time for a little tension to build. If a cuckoo clock is not available or practical, the following alternative props might be considered: (a) a music box about which the leader could build anticipation by describing its lovely music while drawing out the ceremony of winding and opening the box; (b) a jack-in-the-box set to go off at random when the handle is turned; (c) a brightly wrapped box holding what the leader describes as a beautiful surprise, but which the leader does not immediately open (could contain a toy puppy or kitten or a tiny Christmas tree, etc.). In short, any item or device that will build suspense might be used, including, if necessary, an alarm clock or a kitchen timer.

Scripture References: Luke 1:26–56; Isaiah 40:31

Large Economy Size

Motivation: The leader provides instructions and directions as some helpers wheel in an enormous colorfully wrapped box (refrigerator size) mounted on an appliance dolly.

Activity: The leader announces that this particular box is empty (see note in "Materials" section) but invites the children to speculate what might be inside.

Guided Discussion: What might fit in a box like this? (A refrigerator. A stove. A bed. A washing machine. A dryer. Etc.)

Leader Message: Well! Whatever comes in a box this size has got to be *big!* When I see a big package like this I get excited, not so much about what might be inside, but because it helps me think about the special and big present that comes to each and every one of us at Christmas time: the gift of God's wonderful, full, and boundless love. What a joy and blessing! Imagine a package large enough to hold such a present.

Closing Prayer: We thank you, dear God, for the gift of Jesus. Whatever else we may receive, let us never lose sight of this precious gift, a gift that has changed the world. Amen. (The leader may wish to adjust the closing prayer to circumstances suggested in the materials section below.)

Materials: A large, refrigerator-size cardboard box covered with wrapping paper. An appliance dolly and some willing assistants. To safeguard sanctuary flooring or carpet, the dolly should be carefully checked for defective or greasy wheels. A protective "path" of canvas or other material may have to be laid to facilitate wheeling.
(Note: For added effect, if an appropriate event can be arranged, the box might actually contain a large item, such as a plant for the sanctuary, some new chairs for a meeting room, books for the church library, new hymnals, a new refrigerator for the church kitchen, etc. It would be particularly dramatic if only a few mem-

bers of the congregation were aware that the box actually contained a special surprise gift. It might contain something a youth group has worked to raise money for but that has not yet been formally purchased or installed. The reader is invited to consider other possibilities. In a case where the box actually contains a surprise gift, the references above to the empty carton would have to be modified. The message and prayer might also be altered to emphasize sharing or special gifts to the church rather than the theme of God's boundless love. To preface the opening of the package, the leader might say, at the close of the "Leader Message," "Now, I wonder what *is* inside this box. Here's a tag. Can someone read this for us?" A child might read the tag, or the target of the surprise might be called forward to do so; that is, the unsuspecting kitchen manager might be called forward to read the tag, which says, for example, "Here's the new refrigerator you've been dreaming about. Merry Christmas from the Junior High Youth Group!" If the box is to be opened then and there, it will be useful to precut a "door" in the carton, or to cut it so that the box can be "peeled" back, or lifted up and away to reveal the contents.)

Scripture
Reference: Isaiah 9:6

The Good Shepherds

Motivation: The leader displays a shepherd's crook
                and several small balls or fluffs of cotton
                or wool.

Activity: The children are invited to play the role of
                shepherds: herding, protecting, and car-
                ing for these imaginary sheep. After some
                attention the "sheep" are all herded into a
                "barn" (box or bag) and then the leader
                speaks to the children.

Guided
Discussion: What does a shepherd do? (Looks after
                the sheep. Protects them while they sleep.
                Moves them around. Takes them to food
                and water. Keeps them safe.)

Leader
Message: The life of a shepherd is demanding. A
                shepherd must make certain that the
                sheep are fed, watered, and protected.
                Often the shepherd must stay with the
                flock day and night. Shepherding is hard

work and it keeps a person busy. At Christmas time I always think of how the shepherds of old must have marveled when a voice from the heavens told them to leave their sheep and go in search of the baby Jesus. They must have been reluctant to leave their sheep, but the call to Jesus was so powerful that even these hardworking, faithful shepherds could not deny it. Every Christmas, and indeed every single day of our Christian lives, Jesus calls us to stop our work for a moment, lift ourselves above our daily cares and problems, and come to God.

Closing
Prayer:

Dear God, we thank you for the role of shepherds who faithfully care for their flocks. Help us to listen for your word and seek you in the midst of our daily lives. Amen.

Materials:

A shepherd's crook or a stick fashioned to resemble a crook; several cotton balls or fluffs of wool; a small box or bag to serve as a barn.

Scripture Reference:

Luke 2:8–20

Front Page News

Motivation:	The leader displays a newspaper and talks about its various sections (front page, comics, classified ads, sports page, etc.).
Activity:	The children are asked to think about what part of the newspaper is most important.
Guided Discussion:	Which section of the newspaper is the most important? (Various answers, including the front page.)

Leader
Message: I suppose it depends on what information
                 you're seeking. Sometimes at Christ-
                 mastime we get distracted by the ads for
                 toys and other presents. Sometimes, after
                 the big game, we turn right to the sports
                 page for pictures and scores. But most
                 readers would probably agree that the
                 most important part of the paper is the
                 front page. And so (leader brings forth
                 from inside the paper a previously unseen
                 sheet bearing the headline "JESUS IS
                 BORN!" or "JESUS LIVES!") this is how
                 a newspaper for Christmas should look
                 because the message here—that Jesus is
                 born and that he lives—is the most won-
                 derful, most important, and most glorious
                 front page news in the world.

Closing
Prayer: O God, there is so much in our lives to be
                 experienced. Help us to recognize the big-
                 gest news of all. We pray that you may
                 guide us to know the tremendous news of
                 Christmas. In Jesus' name. Amen.

Materials: A regular newspaper or a special sheet
                 with the headline "JESUS IS BORN!" or
                 a similar message. The special sheet
                 should resemble the front page of a news-
                 paper in size and format. It might be pro-
                 duced by handprinting, by the use of
                 stick-on letters, or by having it printed at
                 a local newspaper or a novelty shop that
                 specializes in custom headlines.

Scripture
Reference: Matthew 1:18–25

Take a Hike

Motivation: The leader appears before the group sporting hiking gear: boots, a pack, a walking stick, etc.

Activity: The leader invites the children to come along on a hike, saying that they must first locate a trail. The leader calls the attention of the children to a corner of the sanctuary where a sign saying "trail" is visible. The group relocates to that corner, where they discover the end of a string. With the leader at the head, the group forms a line and follows the string "trail" as it weaves throughout the sanctuary and back to the original gathering spot (where leader first appeared in hiking gear). There the children find a manger scene.

Guided Discussion: Are we the first people to go for a long walk and discover a manger at the end of our journey? (No.) Who else made such a journey? (The shepherds. The wise men.) Were you surprised by what we found? (Yes.)

Leader Message: When the wise men began their journey nearly two thousand years ago, they had a guide, just as we had the string to follow. Their guide was a lovely, bright star, the brightest star anyone had ever seen. They followed the star, not knowing exactly what they would find, but believing it would lead them to a king. Imagine their surprise when their path led not to a fine palace, but to a manger, a stable where animals were kept. There they found a baby, the baby Jesus. Did they turn away disappointed? No. They were not called wise men for nothing. They recognized at once that Jesus was a king and more: the "King of Kings," the "Son of God." They knelt before the baby, offered gifts, and worshiped God and Jesus.

Closing Prayer: Thank you, God, for guiding us to the Lord Jesus. Help us to recognize your love for us and guide our lives to do your will. Amen.

Materials: A "trail" sign, a length of string, and a portable manger scene. The trail should take the leader and the children out of sight of the main sactuary long enough for an assistant quickly to bring the other end of the string to the meeting point while also placing the manger scene in an appropriate spot. The manger scene should be portable and self-contained, since set-up time will be limited. A second assistant or two might be needed to place the manger.

Scripture
Reference: Matthew 2:16–20

Gone, But Not Forgotten

Motivation: The leader displays a few Christmas orna-
                ments.

Activity: The children are invited to examine the
                ornaments and decide what they mean.
                (What do they represent? What do you
                think of when you see them?)

Guided
Discussion: What do these ornaments mean? What do
                you think of when you see them? (Christ-
                mas tree. Christmas. Santa Claus. Pres-
                ents. Bell. Ball. Deer. Sled. Bird. Angel.
                Jesus. God.)

Leader
Message: I'm not surprised that you had different
                answers. The meaning of these ornaments

and of Christmas itself is getting a little mixed up these days. What's more, when Christmas is over—when the day has passed—we usually take down the tree and pack up the ornaments and the tinsel and forget about Christmas until next December. But if we as Christians look around and look closely, we can see many enduring symbols of Christmas and of the realities of Christ's birth and Christ's presence on earth. And I think one of the most special reminders of Christ and Christ's love is right here in front of me. (Addressing the children.) Each of you and every child in this wide world is, for me, a daily reminder that nearly two thousand years ago, Jesus came to us as a child and that he lives forever in the hearts of those who believe in him.

Closing
Prayer: Dear God, let Christmas live in our hearts all year long. Help us to see your love in the daily events of our lives and in our children. Remind us of the power of your love and your sacrifice. Amen.

Materials: Assorted, colorful Christmas ornaments, preferably nonbreakable.

*Scripture
References:*   Ephesians 2:4–10; Philippians 4:8–9

Super Bowl

Motivation:

The leader displays an opaque, covered bowl filled with multicolored scraps of paper. This bowl is labeled "Bowl of Green Paper."

Activity:

The leader invites the children to examine the bowl without opening it and to be prepared to read the sign.

Guided
Discussion:

What does this sign say? (Bowl of Green Paper.) What do you think we will find inside? (Green paper.) Let's take a look. (The leader reaches inside, or allows various children to do so.) What happened? (They aren't green. Different colors. You fooled us. The sign is wrong.) What must I do if I want a bowl of green paper? (Take the other colors out. Separate them.) Let's do that. (The children assist the leader in placing only green paper scraps in the bowl; the others are placed in a paper sack and both the sack and the bowl are placed aside.)

Leader Message:	Christmastime is filled with many bright colors and wonderful sounds: brilliant lights, tall Christmas trees, colorful packages, good things to eat, and lots of Christmas music. After a while Christmas becomes cluttered and confusing. Sometimes we have to sit down and sort things out, much like we sorted through these scraps of paper. Many things have become part of the holiday season since that simple time in a manger so long ago. In some ways it has become a jumble. Every year after Christmas has passed, I find it helpful to sit down and sort out what really happened. When I do that I am able once again to remember the true meaning of Christmas: the wonderful news that Jesus was born and is with us always.
Closing Prayer:	Dear God, we thank you for the beauty of Christmas. We recognize that our world has become complicated and crowded with ideas. Help us to sort out the meaning of Christmas and to see the beauty of your love. Amen.
Materials:	An opaque bowl (preferably of plastic so the children can easily handle it) with a tightly fitting lid. Bits of colored construction paper, including, of course, green along with other bright colors. A paper sack to use for non-green pieces during the sorting exercise.
Scripture Reference:	Matthew 2:16–20